This planner belongs to

_____

Phone Number

_____

Email Address

_____

"Our greatest fear should not be of failure, but of succeeding at something that doesn't really matter." Dwight L. Moody

God's Way to Success Planner

In this planner you will find:

- 1 page for your annual goals
- Daily pages
- Monthly Calendars
- Monthly Income/Expense Sheets
- Monthly task list pages
- Quarterly goal pages
- Quarterly recap pages
- 8 note pages for Brilliant Ideas

Each is straight forward and easy to use.

Neuroscience studies have shown that the act of handwriting your goals rather than typing them significantly increases neural pathways. And writing your goals in general whether typed or handwritten significantly increases your odds of achieving them. There was a reason God told us to write them down.

"Write the vision and make it plain on tablets, that he may run who reads it. For the vision is yet for an appointed time; But at the end it will speak, and it will not lie. Though it tarries, wait for it; Because it will surely come, It will not tarry." Habakkuk 2:2-3

Active faith takes action. As a believer if I were to ask you if you believed the promises of scripture about who God is, what He can do and who He says you are and what you can do, I am certain you would say yes, you believe. Now it is time to for those beliefs to go from passive to active.

God is for you and directing you to "take the land". You will do it step by step walking by faith trusting in God's way and His timing. His plan is best.

"I will not do it all in one year, for the land would become a wilderness, and the wild animals would become too many to control. But I will drive them out a little at a time, until your population has increased enough to fill the land. And I will set your enlarged boundaries from the Red Sea to the Philistine coast, and from the southern deserts as far as the Euphrates River; and I will cause you to defeat the people now living in the land, and you will drive them out ahead of you." Exodus 23:29-31

Annual:
- List your goals and keep them in front of you.
- If you are a visual learner or just creative, find pictures or words from magazines that represent your goals and create a binder or bulletin board so you're reminded of your what and why. Pull this out during your prayer time and discuss your goals with God.

Quarterly:
- List your goals and keep them in front of you.
- Do a quarterly recap

Monthly:
- Create task list to be done to stay on track with your goals
- Review previous months task list. Transfer any undone tasks over.
- Pray and reflect on the reasons why you didn't accomplish the tasks, then recalibrate.

Weekly:
- Review progress and add action steps to planner.
- If you are doing accountability, keep in touch with partner/group/coach via email, phone or in person.

Daily Planner Pages

Set aside some time on Sunday nights or first thing Monday morning to plan your week.

Schedule: Fill in your meetings and appointments first so you know when you will have time to work on the tasks that will advance your goals.

To-Do: Refer back to the monthly task list and add tasks.

Outfits: To make your busy schedule a little smoother determine what you will wear when you fill in your planner for the week. Look at the week, the weather forecast, where you are going and what you have to do. The less decisions you have to make in the moment the less anxiety you'll have and you save your brain power for more important decisions. Then all you'll need to do is put out the clothes each night that you've already decided on. Bonus: You'll be your own wardrobe stylist. As you put together outfits and write them down, you'll create a record of what items you have worn together before so you end up being more fashionable and quicker when it comes to getting ready each day.

Dinner: Deciding what you'll make for dinner at the beginning of the week helps with two very important things- grocery shopping and eating healthier which also advance at least two potential goals; budget and health.

Accountability:
The American Society of Training and Development (ASTD) did a study on completing goals and found the following statistics:
The probability of completing a goal if:
- You have an idea or a goal: 10%
- You consciously decide you will do it: 25%
- You decide when you will do it: 40%
- You plan how you will do it: 50%
- You commit to someone you will do it: 65%
- You have a specific accountability appointment with a person you've committed to: **95%**

If you are continually struggling to accomplish a task or a goal, maybe it's time to ask for help.

"Plans fail for lack of counsel, but with many advisers they succeed." Proverbs 15:22

Last Thoughts

Remember as you seek God's face and set out to accomplish your goals to enjoy each day. Don't wait until you reach each goal to be happy. Life is truly about the journey.

May the LORD bless you
and protect you.
May the LORD smile on you
and be gracious to you.
May the LORD show you his favor
and give you his peace.
Numbers 6:24-26

For more biblical planner and goal setting resources go to:

www.jenniferleesmith.com or www.Godswaytosuccess.com

ANNUAL GOALS

1ST QUARTER GOALS

January

SUNDAY	MONDAY	TUESDAY	WEDNESDAY	THURSDAY	FRIDAY	SATURDAY
			1	2	3	4
5	6	7	8	9	10	11
12	13	14	15	16	17	18
19	20	21	22	23	24	25
26	27	28	29	30	31	

Teach us to number our days and recognize how few they are;
help us to spend them as we should.
Psalm 90:12

January Monthly Tasks

Income	Expenses

Today's Plan

Wednesday, January 1, 2020

To Do:

Schedule:

Dinner:

Notes:

Outfit:

Today's Plan

Thursday, January 2, 2020

To Do:

Schedule:

Dinner:

Notes:

Outfit:

Today's Plan

Friday, January 3, 2020

To Do:

Schedule:

Dinner:

Notes:

Outfit:

Today's Plan

Saturday, January 4, 2020

To Do:

Schedule:

Dinner:

Notes:

Outfit:

Today's Plan

Sunday, January 5, 2020

To Do:

Schedule:

Dinner:

Notes:

Outfit:

Today's Plan

Monday, January 6, 2020

To Do:

Schedule:

Dinner:

Notes:

Outfit:

Today's Plan

Tuesday, January 7, 2020

To Do:

Schedule:

Dinner:

Notes:

Outfit:

Today's Plan

Wednesday, January 8, 2020

To Do:

Schedule:

Dinner:

Notes:

Outfit:

Today's Plan

Thursday, January 9, 2020

To Do:

Schedule:

Dinner:

Notes:

Outfit:

Today's Plan

Friday, January 10, 2020

To Do:

Schedule:

Dinner:

Notes:

Outfit:

Today's Plan

Saturday, January 11, 2020

To Do:

Schedule:

Dinner:

Notes:

Outfit:

Today's Plan

Sunday, January 12, 2020

To Do:

Schedule:

Dinner:

Notes:

Outfit:

Today's Plan

Monday, January 13, 2020

To Do:

Schedule:

Dinner:

Notes:

Outfit:

Today's Plan

Tuesday, January 14, 2020

To Do:

Schedule:

Dinner:

Notes:

Outfit:

Today's Plan

Wednesday, January 15, 2020

To Do:

Schedule:

Dinner:

Notes:

Outfit:

Today's Plan

Thursday, January 16, 2020

To Do:

Schedule:

Dinner:

Notes:

Outfit:

Today's Plan

Friday, January 17, 2020

To Do:

Schedule:

Dinner:

Notes:

Outfit:

Today's Plan

Saturday, January 18, 2020

To Do:

Schedule:

Dinner:

Notes:

Outfit:

Today's Plan

Sunday, January 19, 2020

To Do:

Schedule:

Dinner:

Notes:

Outfit:

Today's Plan

Monday, January 20, 2020

To Do:

Schedule:

Dinner:

Notes:

Outfit:

Today's Plan

Tuesday, January 21, 2020

To Do:

Schedule:

Dinner:

Notes:

Outfit:

Today's Plan

Wednesday, January 22, 2020

To Do:

Schedule:

Dinner:

Notes:

Outfit:

Today's Plan

Thursday, January 23, 2020

To Do:

Schedule:

Dinner:

Notes:

Outfit:

Today's Plan

Friday, January 24, 2020

To Do:

Schedule:

Dinner:

Notes:

Outfit:

Today's Plan

Saturday, January 25, 2020

To Do:

Schedule:

Dinner:

Notes:

Outfit:

Today's Plan

Sunday, January 26, 2020

To Do:

Schedule:

Dinner:

Notes:

Outfit:

Today's Plan

Monday, January 27, 2020

To Do:

Schedule:

Dinner:

Notes:

Outfit:

Today's Plan

Tuesday, January 28, 2020

To Do:

Schedule:

Dinner:

Notes:

Outfit:

Today's Plan

Wednesday, January 29, 2020

To Do:

Schedule:

Dinner:

Notes:

Outfit:

Today's Plan

Thursday, January 30, 2020

To Do:

Schedule:

Dinner:

Notes:

Outfit:

Today's Plan

Friday, January 31, 2020

To Do:

Schedule:

Dinner:

Notes:

Outfit:

February

SUNDAY	MONDAY	TUESDAY	WEDNESDAY	THURSDAY	FRIDAY	SATURDAY
						1
2	3	4	5	6	7	8
9	10	11	12	13	14	15
16	17	18	19	20	21	22
23	24	25	26	27	28	29

Teach us to number our days and recognize how few they are;
help us to spend them as we should.
Psalm 90:12

February Monthly Tasks

Income	Expenses

Today's Plan

Saturday, February 1, 2020

To Do:

Schedule:

Dinner:

Notes:

Outfit:

Today's Plan

Sunday, February 2, 2020

To Do:

Schedule:

Dinner:

Notes:

Outfit:

Today's Plan

Monday, February 3, 2020

To Do:

Schedule:

Dinner:

Notes:

Outfit:

Today's Plan

Tuesday, February 4, 2020

To Do:

Schedule:

Dinner:

Notes:

Outfit:

Today's Plan

Wednesday, February 5, 2020

To Do:

Schedule:

Dinner:

Notes:

Outfit:

Today's Plan

Thursday, February 6, 2020

To Do:

Schedule:

Dinner:

Notes:

Outfit:

Today's Plan

Friday, February 7, 2020

To Do:

Schedule:

Dinner:

Notes:

Outfit:

Today's Plan

Saturday, February 8, 2020

To Do:

Schedule:

Dinner:

Notes:

Outfit:

Today's Plan

Sunday, February 9, 2020

To Do:

Schedule:

Dinner:

Notes:

Outfit:

Today's Plan

Monday, February 10, 2020

To Do:

Schedule:

Dinner:

Notes:

Outfit:

Today's Plan

Tuesday, February 11, 2020

To Do:

Schedule:

Dinner:

Notes:

Outfit:

Today's Plan

Wednesday, February 12, 2020

To Do:

Schedule:

Dinner:

Notes:

Outfit:

Today's Plan

Thursday, February 13, 2020

To Do:

Schedule:

Dinner:

Notes:

Outfit:

Today's Plan

Friday, February 14, 2020

To Do:

Schedule:

Dinner:

Notes:

Outfit:

Today's Plan

Saturday, February 15, 2020

To Do:

Schedule:

Dinner:

Notes:

Outfit:

Today's Plan

Sunday, February 16, 2020

To Do:

Schedule:

Dinner:

Notes:

Outfit:

Today's Plan

Monday, February 17, 2020

To Do:

Schedule:

Dinner:

Notes:

Outfit:

Today's Plan

Tuesday, February 18, 2020

To Do:

Schedule:

Dinner:

Notes:

Outfit:

Today's Plan

Wednesday, February 19, 2020

To Do:

Schedule:

Dinner:

Notes:

Outfit:

Today's Plan

Thursday, February 20, 2020

To Do:

Schedule:

Dinner:

Notes:

Outfit:

Today's Plan

Friday, February 21, 2020

To Do:

Schedule:

Dinner:

Notes:

Outfit:

Today's Plan

Saturday, February 22, 2020

To Do:

Schedule:

Dinner:

Notes:

Outfit:

Today's Plan

Sunday, February 23, 2020

To Do:

Schedule:

Dinner:

Notes:

Outfit:

Today's Plan

Monday, February 24, 2020

To Do:

Schedule:

Dinner:

Notes:

Outfit:

Today's Plan

Tuesday, February 25, 2020

To Do:

Schedule:

Dinner:

Notes:

Outfit:

Today's Plan

Wednesday, February 26, 2020

To Do:

Schedule:

Dinner:

Notes:

Outfit:

Today's Plan

Thursday, February 27, 2020

To Do:

Schedule:

Dinner:

Notes:

Outfit:

Today's Plan

Friday, February 28, 2020

To Do:

Schedule:

Dinner:

Notes:

Outfit:

Today's Plan

Saturday, February 29, 2020

To Do:

Schedule:

Dinner:

Notes:

Outfit:

March

SUNDAY	MONDAY	TUESDAY	WEDNESDAY	THURSDAY	FRIDAY	SATURDAY
1	2	3	4	5	6	7
8	9	10	11	12	13	14
15	16	17	18	19	20	21
22	23	24	25	26	27	28
29	30	31				

Teach us to number our days and recognize how few they are;
help us to spend them as we should.
Psalm 90:12

March Monthly Tasks

Income	Expenses

Today's Plan

Sunday, March 1, 2020

To Do:

Schedule:

Dinner:

Notes:

Outfit:

Today's Plan

Monday, March 2, 2020

To Do:

Schedule:

Dinner:

Notes:

Outfit:

Today's Plan

Tuesday, March 3, 2020

To Do:

Schedule:

Dinner:

Notes:

Outfit:

Today's Plan

Wednesday, March 4, 2020

To Do:

Schedule:

Dinner:

Notes:

Outfit:

Today's Plan

Thursday, March 5, 2020

To Do:

Schedule:

Dinner:

Notes:

Outfit:

Today's Plan

Friday, March 6, 2020

To Do:

Schedule:

Dinner:

Notes:

Outfit:

Today's Plan

Saturday, March 7, 2020

To Do:

Schedule:

Dinner:

Notes:

Outfit:

Today's Plan

Sunday, March 8, 2020

To Do:

Schedule:

Dinner:

Notes:

Outfit:

Today's Plan

Monday, March 9, 2020

To Do:

Schedule:

Dinner:

Notes:

Outfit:

Today's Plan

Tuesday, March 10, 2020

To Do:

Schedule:

Dinner:

Notes:

Outfit:

Today's Plan

Wednesday, March 11, 2020

To Do:

Schedule:

Dinner:

Notes:

Outfit:

Today's Plan

Thursday, March 12, 2020

To Do:

Schedule:

Dinner:

Notes:

Outfit:

Today's Plan

Friday, March 13, 2020

To Do:

Schedule:

Dinner:

Notes:

Outfit:

Today's Plan

Saturday, March 14, 2020

To Do:

Schedule:

Dinner:

Notes:

Outfit:

Today's Plan

Sunday, March 15, 2020

To Do:

Schedule:

Dinner:

Notes:

Outfit:

Today's Plan

Monday, March 16, 2020

To Do:

Schedule:

Dinner:

Notes:

Outfit:

Today's Plan

Tuesday, March 17, 2020

To Do:

Schedule:

Dinner:

Notes:

Outfit:

Today's Plan

Wednesday, March 18, 2020

To Do:

Schedule:

Dinner:

Notes:

Outfit:

Today's Plan

Thursday, March 19, 2020

To Do:

Schedule:

Dinner:

Notes:

Outfit:

Today's Plan

Friday, March 20, 2020

To Do:

Schedule:

Dinner:

Notes:

Outfit:

Today's Plan

Saturday, March 21, 2020

To Do:

Schedule:

Dinner:

Notes:

Outfit:

Today's Plan

Sunday, March 22, 2020

To Do:

Schedule:

Dinner:

Notes:

Outfit:

Today's Plan

Monday, March 23, 2020

To Do:

Schedule:

Dinner:

Notes:

Outfit:

Today's Plan

Tuesday, March 24, 2020

To Do:

Schedule:

Dinner:

Notes:

Outfit:

Today's Plan

Wednesday, March 25, 2020

To Do:

Schedule:

Dinner:

Notes:

Outfit:

Today's Plan

Thursday, March 26, 2020

To Do:

Schedule:

Dinner:

Notes:

Outfit:

Today's Plan

Friday, March 27, 2020

To Do:

Schedule:

Dinner:

Notes:

Outfit:

Today's Plan

Saturday, March 28, 2020

To Do:

Schedule:

Dinner:

Notes:

Outfit:

Today's Plan

Sunday, March 29, 2020

To Do:

Schedule:

Dinner:

Notes:

Outfit:

Today's Plan

Monday, March 30, 2020

To Do:

Schedule:

Dinner:

Notes:

Outfit:

Today's Plan

Tuesday, March 31, 2020

To Do:

Schedule:

Dinner:

Notes:

Outfit:

Quarterly Recap

- What was the wisest thing you did this quarter?

- What 3 things happened that disappointed you?

- List 3 great things that happened:

- List 3 things you could have done better:

- Pick 1 act of service you did that helped another person, glorified God and blessed you:

Brilliant Ideas

Brilliant Ideas

Brilliant Ideas

Brilliant Ideas

Brilliant Ideas

Brilliant Ideas

Brilliant Ideas

Brilliant Ideas

For more biblical planner and goal setting resources go to:

www.jenniferleesmith.com or www.Godswaytosuccess.com

Made in the USA
Coppell, TX
03 January 2020